Sound Trackers

1990s Pop

SOUND TRACKERS - 1990s POP
was produced by

David West Children's Books
7 Princeton Court
55 Felsham Road
London SW15 1AZ

Designer: Rob Shone
Picture Research: Fiona Thorne
Editor: James Pickering

First published in Great Britain in 2002 by
Heinemann Library, Halley Court, Jordan Hill, Oxford OX2 8EJ, a division of
Reed Educational and Professional Publishing Limited.

OXFORD MELBOURNE AUCKLAND
JOHANNESBURG BLANTYRE GABORONE
IBADAN PORTSMOUTH (NH) USA CHICAGO

06 05 04 03 02
10 9 8 7 6 5 4 3 2 1

ISBN 0 431 09113 7 (HB)
ISBN 0 431 09120 X (PB)

British Library Cataloguing in Publication Data

Brunning, Bob
1990s pop. - (Soundtrackers)
1. Popular music - 1991-2000 - Juvenile literature
2. Musicians - Juvenile literature
I. Title II. Nineteen hundred and nineties pop
III. Nineteen nineties pop
781.6'4

Printed and bound in Italy

SOUND TRACKERS

1990s Pop

Bob Brunning

CONTENTS

On these discs is a selection of the artist's recordings. Many of these albums are available on CD. If they are not, many of the tracks from them can be found on compilation CDs.

The MTV awards are a popular fixture on the pop music calendar each year.

These boxes give you extra information about the artists and their times.

Some contain anecdotes about the artists themselves or about the people who helped their careers or, occasionally, about those who exploited them.

Others provide historical facts about the music, lifestyle, fans, fads and fashions of the day.

INTRODUCTION

Pop music had been around for a long time by the 1990s. It was becoming increasingly difficult for musicians to come up with any new ideas, and much of the music of that decade owed a huge debt to the fashions of the past. There were the boy bands, who revived a trend that had been out of fashion since the '70s, and Madonna was a vast influence on the female singers and girl groups of the '90s. If the 1980s had been dominated by synthesizers and drum machines, the '90s saw the return of guitar bands, spearheaded by the Britpop sounds of Blur, Oasis and Suede.

The Icelandic singer Björk took the charts by storm with her 1993 album 'Debut', with its blend of dance music and strident vocals. Her other albums included 'Post' and 'Telegram'. The picture above shows how she appeared on her 1997 album 'Homogenic'.

But there was some great original music too. Artists such as Björk used modern recording technology to create new sounds and explore new musical territory. And '80s favourites, such as Sting, George Michael, U2 and R.E.M., filled stadiums with their brand of rock which was bold and experimental, but easy on the ear.

The future of songwriting was in good hands too, courtesy of Noel Gallagher and Damon Albarn. Even the boy bands and girl groups, who were condemned as lightweight and manufactured, came up with songs that will still be sung long into the future. And the '90s teen idols Robbie Williams and Ronan Keating have matured into sophisticated entertainers, reaching new heights in the 21st century.

ALL SAINTS

In the early 1960s, the Beatles were popular with all the family. The Rolling Stones were the exact opposite – the bad boys of pop. 30 years later, All Saints were promoted as the harder, grittier version of the Spice Girls.

A BAND TO BE TAKEN SERIOUSLY

There were marked similarities between the two girl groups. All Saints were two brunettes, one blonde and an Afro-Caribbean, and they were all singers (not instrumentalists). Only a ginger singer was missing. But they made much of their original songwriting skills, and they were a street band, composed of four musicians, not products of stage school and the modelling circuit. Shaznay Lewis and Melanie Blatt began recording together in a studio in All Saints Road, London, in 1993.

'All Saints' 1997

'Saints And Sinners' 2000

All Saints were overwhelmed by their Brit Award success in 1997.

A LONG WAY TO THE TOP

Their first single in 1995 was a failure, and they were promptly dumped by their record label. Uncowed, they recruited Canadian sisters Nicole and Natalie Appleton to make All Saints a quartet. Their manager, John Benson, secured them a new deal, and enlisted the help of top producers Nellee Hooper and Cameron McVey. 'I Know Where It's At' hit No. 4 in the UK charts and launched the group throughout Europe and Asia.

A STRING OF HITS

All Saints' next single, penned by Shaznay, was a monster hit. The tale of a doomed love affair, 'Never Ever' won them a Brit Award and much respect from fans and critics alike. Two more chart-toppers followed in 1998. Their single 'Pure Shores' was the biggest hit of 2000, but all was not well with All Saints.

Shaznay Lewis was the chief songwriter for All Saints.

FROZEN OUT

Their 2001 European tour was cancelled, and the band was officially put on ice, owing to business disagreements. But Melanie Blatt has not ruled out a future reunion for All Saints – as long as the price is right!

HONEST

While Shaznay Lewis was in the studio, writing material for All Saints, the other three group members starred in a wacky crime comedy film, called 'Honest'. The movie was the first by director David A. Stewart, better known as half of the '80s duo the Eurythmics. The movie wasn't the box-office smash they had hoped for, and its relative failure might have hastened All Saints' split.

'Honest' was premièred at the 2000 Cannes film festival.

BLUR

The career of the 'Britpop' band Blur nearly stalled before the '90s were truly underway. It took them five years of hard work before they hit the top of the charts.

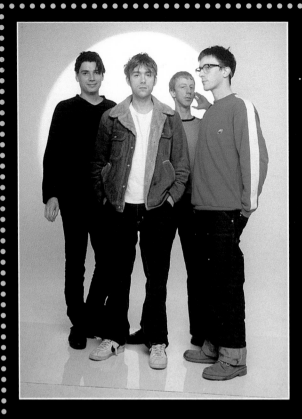

'Leisure' 1991
'Modern Life Is Rubbish' 1993
'Parklife' 1994

'The Great Escape' 1995
'Blur' 1997
'13' 1999

EARLY STRUGGLE

Damon Albarn, Graham Coxon and Alex James formed Seymour in London in 1989, with drummer Dave Rowntree joining the line-up soon after. They signed with the Food label, who suggested they change their name, and released their first album 'Leisure'. Many critics thought the band sounded too old-fashioned, and Blur struggled to adopt a harder sound. Their second album, 'Modern Life Is Rubbish', was initially rejected by Food, so it was back to the studio again. Food was eventually satisfied, but Blur's American label was not. The band was exhausted when the record was eventually released, but they learned from their mistakes, and returned in 1994 with one of the biggest albums of the '90s.

Blur celebrated their success at the 1995 Brit Awards.

BLUR v OASIS

The album was 'Parklife', which entered the UK chart at No. 1, and catapulted the band to stardom. It gave them the hit singles 'Girls And Boys' and 'To The End', and seemed to pave the way for a new movement of guitar bands, labelled 'Britpop'. The media were determined to fuel a rivalry between Blur and the northern act Oasis, and Blur eagerly rose to the bait, releasing the single 'Country House' on the same day as Oasis's 'Roll With It' in a battle for the No. 1 slot. Oasis won hands down, and Blur went on tour to promote their next album, 'The Great Escape'.

ELASTICA

Elastica was one of the leading Britpop bands to emerge in the early 1990s. Lead-singer Justine Frischmann was romantically linked with Blur's Damon Albarn, just as both bands were high in the charts. Elastica's self-titled album was said to be the fastest-selling debut in chart history, but they failed to build on this success. The second album, 'The Menace' only appeared in 2000, six years after its predecessor.

Justine Frischmann (second from right) was in Suede at the start of her career.

TIME OFF

Blur almost split in 1996, but decided instead to take a year off to recuperate. They returned with their fifth album, which gave them another No. 1 single, 'Beetlebum'. They even enjoyed some long-awaited success in the USA, before Damon Albarn took a break from Blur to play with the 'virtual hip-hop' act Gorillaz.

Damon Albarn is an accomplished songwriter.

BOYZONE

The phenomenon of the boy band was not new to the '90s. The 1970s had seen some enormously popular boy bands, such as the Jackson 5 and the Osmonds, but this style of singing and dancing group had gone out of fashion in the '80s. But the huge success of Britain's Take That opened the floodgates for dozens of boy bands. Ireland gave the world Boyzone.

AUDITION TIME

Like so many other acts of the '90s, the idea of Boyzone was conceived by an ambitious manager, in this case Louis Walsh, who advertised for five male singers and dancers (just like Take That). 300 hopefuls were boiled down to five lucky winners – lead singer Ronan Keating, plus Mikey Graham, Stephen Gately, Shane Lynch and Keith Duffy. Their first singles were cover versions of popular 1970s hits.

Boyzone covered 'Father And Son' by Cat Stevens.

'Said And Done' 1995
'A Different Beat' 1996

'Where We Belong' 1998
'By Request' 1999

ORIGINAL MATERIAL

Boyzone's renditions of the Detroit Spinners' 'Working My Way Back To You' and the Osmonds' 'Love Me For A Reason' both made the Irish top 3, and the Bee Gees' 'Words' hit UK No. 1. But Boyzone wisely realised that they needed original material if they were going to last. They hired Take That songwriter Ray Hedges, and Boyzone's first original single 'Key To My Life' topped the UK chart, as did their debut album 'Said And Done'. At last, Take That had a serious rival for the title of top boy band.

Ronan hit No. 1 with 'Life Is A Rollercoaster'.

WESTLIFE

Ronan Keating proved himself to be a clever businessman when he was introduced to fellow Dubliners Westlife. He offered to become the group's co-manager, despite their obvious threat to Boyzone's popularity. Westlife's first single 'Flying Without Wings' entered the chart at No. 1 in 1999, and they repeated this success with 'Seasons In The Sun', 'Swear It Again' and their self-titled first album, 'Westlife'.

Boyzone's manager Louis Walsh introduced Westlife to Ronan Keating.

Boyzone's stage show was expertly choreographed.

TIME TO GROW UP

The members of Boyzone are proud of the hard work they have put into their music. They became the first act in chart history to hit the top 3 with their first 14 singles. As they grew up, they managed that most difficult feat for a boy band – they began to be taken seriously by their musical peers. As the new millennium dawned, the group members developed solo careers, and Ronan Keating hit No. 1 with 'When You Say Nothing At All'.

EAST 17

All Saints wasn't the only '90s group to name itself after an area of London. One of the biggest boy bands came from Walthamstow – its postcode is East 17.

'Walthamstow' 1993
'Steam' 1995

'Around The World: The Journey So Far' 1996

A CHANGE OF STYLE

Tony Mortimer, Brian Harvey, Terry Coldwell and John Hendy hooked up with the aim of emulating the best American rap and hip-hop acts of the day. But East London isn't downtown L.A., and it was only when they changed their sound, to appeal to the teen-market that success came their way. Their good looks helped, and East 17 was signed by Tom Watkins, who had launched Bros and the Pet Shop Boys in the '80s.

OVERSEAS SUCCESS

In 1992, East 17's first single, 'House Of Love' shot into the UK top 10, and the band found themselves darlings of the tabloid press. A critical panning didn't stop their debut album 'Walthamstow' from racing up the charts, as new fans in Australia and the Far East discovered the band.

IN CONCERT

East 17 struggled to gain respect amongst the music press as they played to arenas packed with swooning teenage girls, accompanied by their grumpy boyfriends. They achieved the coveted Christmas No. 1 slot with 'Stay Another Day' in 1994, even playing their own musical instruments!

SONG AND DANCE

Boy and girl bands depend heavily on choreography (dance arrangements) in their stage shows. Music critics tend to dismiss these bands as lightweight and manufactured, but you don't look that good without a lot of skill and practice. The soul acts of the 1960s and '70s were amongst the first to accompany their songs with complex dance routines. Boyzone were very influenced by the Jackson 5, while East 17 paid tribute to American street acts, both in their dance and clothing. And if you think it looks easy, just try singing and dancing at the same time, without losing your breath!

N'Sync is an American boy band.

East 17 was proud of its East London roots.

WHOOPS!

But East 17 was not destined to stay in the public eye for much longer. Brian Harvey foolishly endorsed the use of the illegal drug Ecstasy in an interview, and was thrown out of the band. Some fans hoped East 17 could survive without him, but the damage was done, and guitar bands now reigned supreme in the charts.

East 17's fans copied their way of dressing.

13

HANSON

When no fewer than five record labels turn you down in succession, surely it's time to give up your ambition to be the next pop sensation. Not brothers Isaac, Taylor and Zac Hanson – showing indomitable spirit, the trio from Tulsa, Oklahoma simply would not give up.

'Middle Of Nowhere' 1997
'Snowed In' 1997
'3 Car Garage' 1998

'Live From Albertane' 1998
'This Time Around' 2000

GOING IT ALONE

The singing brothers muscled in on music lawyer Christopher Sabec and sang for him. He agreed to manage them and touted tapes of the group around several record companies. As no one was willing to sign Hanson, they decided to record an independent album, 'Boomerang'. The single 'MMMBop' won them a contract with Mercury Records.

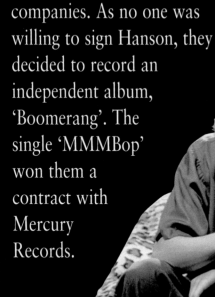

Hanson first performed at school.

POWERFUL BACKING

Mercury put their full weight behind Hanson, and in 1997 the group happily watched the album 'Middle Of Nowhere' and 'MMMBop' storm up the US charts. The three Hanson boys were suddenly the biggest teen sensation in America.

'Middle Of Nowhere' was one of the biggest-selling albums of 1997.

COOL YULE

The boys quickly recorded a new album for the lucrative Christmas market, 'Snowed In', and cleverly re-released their earlier independent recordings. They also captured the excitement and intensity of their live performances with a recording from one of their concerts, 'Live From Albertane'.

BOYS TO MEN

Hanson realized the need to reach out beyond the teenage audience and wisely took time off to produce a more mature record. After a long break, they emerged with 'This Time Around' in 2000, which raised its hat to the heavy sounds which dominated the charts. Let's see if Hanson can repeat its success in the new millennium.

Isaac was 16, Taylor 13 and Zac only 11 at the time of their debut album.

CHILD STARS

There can't be many children who haven't dreamed of being a pop star. But fame can be short-lived. Frankie Lymon was only 13 when he hit the top of the chart with his band the Teenagers in 1956. But at 14 Frankie's voice had broken, and his fame was slipping away. His solo career without the Teenagers stalled, and Frankie lapsed into heroin addiction. He was found dead in 1968, aged just 25.

Frankie Lymon and the Teenagers' biggest hit was 'Why Do Fools Fall In Love'.

OASIS

You can choose your friends, but you can't choose your relations, as the saying goes. When Liam Gallagher invited his brother Noel to join his band, could he have known that this was the start of one of the most bitter, turbulent but inspired relationships in pop history? Some would say that this tension was the secret of Oasis's success.

TAKING THE REINS

Liam Gallagher formed Oasis in Manchester with Paul 'Bonehead' Arthurs, Paul McGuigan and Tony McCarroll, but the band was going nowhere fast. Brother Noel had already experienced life on the road, as a guitar technician for the Inspiral Carpets, when Liam offered him a place in the band. Noel agreed to join on one condition – he insisted on full creative control, including writing all their songs. After a year of intensive rehearsal, Oasis was signed by Alan McGee, the head of Creation Records.

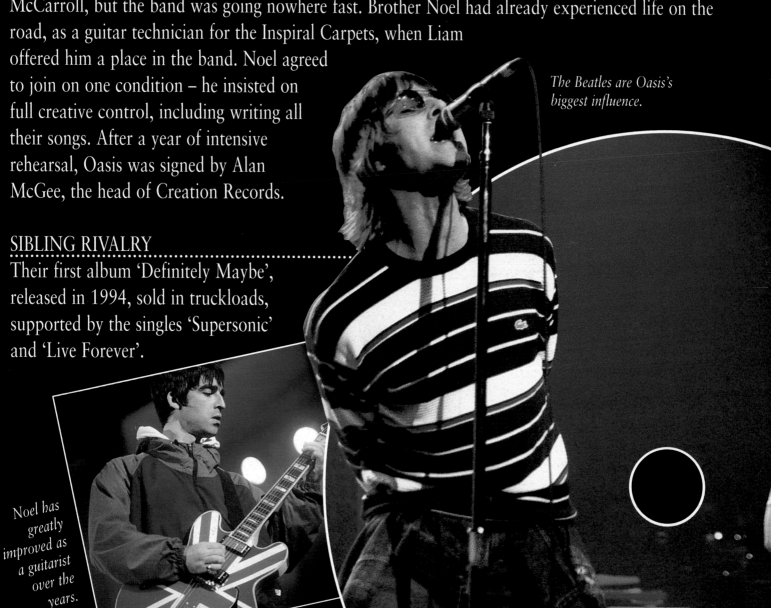

The Beatles are Oasis's biggest influence.

SIBLING RIVALRY

Their first album 'Definitely Maybe', released in 1994, sold in truckloads, supported by the singles 'Supersonic' and 'Live Forever'.

Noel has greatly improved as a guitarist over the years.

'Definitely Maybe' 1994
'(What's The Story) Morning Glory' 1995

'Be Here Now' 1997
'Standing On The Shoulder Of Giants' 2000

TROUBLE AND STRIFE

Noel Gallagher has blamed many of Oasis's troubles on the women around the band. Noel dedicated the love song 'Wonderwall' to his wife Meg Matthews, and Liam had a passionate but stormy marriage to Patsy Kensit. But neither brother got on with the other's wife, and both marriages ended in divorce. Noel has settled into a quiet life in the country and Liam has started a family with Nicole Appleton of All Saints. Oasis has never been so happy.

Noel with Meg (left) and Liam with Patsy (right).

The band was one of the only new British acts to find fame in America during the '90s, but trouble was brewing. Noel and Liam refused to conduct joint interviews because they always ended up quarrelling, and a counterfeit recording of the brothers fighting sold thousands of copies.

SPOILING IT ALL

'(What's The Story) Morning Glory' was Oasis's finest hour. Released in 1995, it quickly became the second-biggest British album in history. Noel was hailed as the major songwriter of the day, and the band embarked on an important US tour, but fighting got in the way again. Oasis lost a lot of respect, and many American fans, when the tour was abandoned, and a split seemed certain. The band retreated to lick its wounds, and took several months to record the follow-up, 'Be Here Now'. The album sold well, but many people felt that it was self-indulgent and over the top, and yet another tour collapsed, partly because of Liam's heavy drinking.

MATURING AT LAST

To the surprise of many, Oasis seemed to grow up in the new millennium. The Gallaghers finally made peace with one another, and even managed to complete a US tour in 2001. They also played some triumphant shows at home, to celebrate the tenth anniversary of the band (even though Noel and Liam are now the only original members). For a band which has nearly split so many times, Oasis looks set to have a very bright future.

PULP

There cannot be another band in chart history which has taken so long to reach the top. For the first twelve years of its existence, Pulp remained in almost total obscurity, until the music press picked up on an independent single, and the band was hailed an overnight success. It must have been satisfying for Jarvis Cocker, the only band member to hang on since Pulp's first gig in 1978.

FALSE START

Jarvis founded Arabicus Pulp at school, and after a handful of shows, he shortened the band's name and arranged a recording session. The results impressed BBC Radio 1 DJ John Peel, and he invited Pulp to perform on his show. Instead of the session leading to a record deal and instant stardom, Pulp's appearance led nowhere. The entire band abandoned Jarvis in 1982.

'Different Class' entered the UK chart at No. 1.

FALL FROM GRACE

Jarvis formed a new Pulp at university and, at last, he landed a record deal in 1984. But the album 'It' wasn't a success, and the band was re-arranged once more. Jarvis was badly injured in 1985, when he fell from a balcony, while trying to impress a girl, and Pulp foundered once more.

Pulp is influenced by David Bowie and Roxy Music.

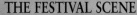

THE FESTIVAL SCENE

Pulp sealed its success at the 1995 Glastonbury rock festival in South West England. The band accepted a headlining slot, when the Stone Roses were forced to pull out at the last minute. Pulp was enthusiastically greeted by the crowd, and Jarvis turned out his best performance to date. Glastonbury has been taking place most summers since the 1970s, and attracts huge numbers of fans, who come from all over the world to see new and established acts.

Glastonbury is famous for its happy atmosphere.

'Separations' 1992
'His 'N' Hers' 1994

'Different Class' 1995
'This Is Hardcore' 1998
'Pulp' 2001

FAME AT LAST

Jarvis found a soulmate in Russell Senior, and the two of them developed the band while Jarvis studied filmmaking. An album recorded in 1989, 'Separations', was finally released three years later, and the press picked up on the single 'My Legendary Girlfriend'. A major record deal followed with Island, and Pulp started to sell serious amounts of records. The hits kept on coming throughout the late '90s – the singles 'Babies' and 'Common People' and the albums 'His 'N' Hers', 'Different Class' and 'This Is Hardcore' to name just a few. The gangly Jarvis suddenly found himself an unlikely pin-up and a popular contributor to TV chat shows and panel games. But Jarvis is also a serious and thoughtful songwriter, and one of the true originals to emerge from the '90s Britpop scene. It was worth the wait!

R.E.M.

Warner Brothers had high hopes for R.E.M. at the beginning of the 1990s. Bill Berry, Peter Buck, Mike Mills and Michael Stipe had been playing together for a decade, to steadily larger audiences, and their last album, 'Green', had sold well. Most bands would have hit the road, but not R.E.M.

'Murmur' 1983
'Reckoning' 1984
'Fables Of The Reconstruction' 1985
'Life's Rich Pageant' 1986
'Document' 1987
'Green' 1988

'Out Of Time' 1991
'Automatic For The People' 1992
'Monster' 1994
'New Adventures In Hi-Fi' 1996
'Up' 1998
'Reveal' 2001

OUT OF BREATH

After releasing five independent albums, R.E.M. signed to Warner Brothers in 1988 for a reputed seven figure sum. But eight years of non-stop touring had left the band exhausted, and R.E.M. firmly refused to go on the road to promote its 1991 album, 'Out Of Time'. Despite this, the album entered the UK and US charts at No. 1, and the singles 'Radio Song', 'Shiny, Happy People' and 'Losing My Religion' became anthems for the new decade. Michael Stipe's pure vocals and Peter Buck's jangly guitar and mandolin dominated the album, with fine songwriting contributions from the whole band.

CAREER HIGH

Many critics regard 'Automatic For The People' as R.E.M.'s greatest album, and it was another huge hit, although the band still refused to go on tour. The singles 'Drive' and 'Man On The Moon' cemented R.E.M.'s reputation as the most radio-friendly band of the decade, but they changed their sound radically for the next album, 'Monster'.

R.E.M. formed in the college town of Athens, Georgia.

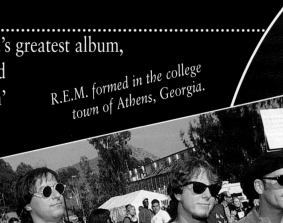

ONE THING AFTER ANOTHER

The album was heavier and louder than anything R.E.M. had produced before, but it won over new fans, who had dismissed the band as too commercial.

THE INDIE SOUND

These days, there's so much competition in the music business, that a deal with a major record label is almost impossible to find. R.E.M., like Oasis and Pulp, weren't content to wait around to be discovered – they recorded a string of independent singles and albums, before Warner Brothers snapped them up. 'Radio Free Europe' was their first single, which became a favourite on American college radio, despite its rarity – only 1,000 copies were pressed. The band toured relentlessly, and built up a loyal fan base, long before they found international fame in the '90s.

R.E.M's first five albums were on the independent I.R.S. label.

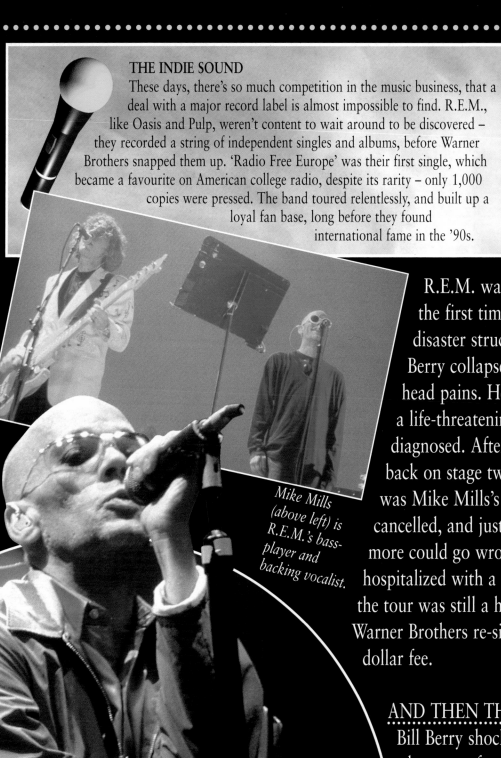

Mike Mills (above left) is R.E.M.'s bass-player and backing vocalist.

R.E.M. was even ready to tour again, for the first time for seven years, but near disaster struck on a date in Switzerland. Bill Berry collapsed on the drum stool with severe head pains. He was rushed to hospital, where a life-threatening brain aneurysm was diagnosed. After emergency surgery, Bill was back on stage two months later, but this time it was Mike Mills's turn to fall ill. More dates were cancelled, and just when it looked like nothing more could go wrong, Michael Stipe was hospitalized with a stomach complaint. Surprisingly, the tour was still a huge financial success, and Warner Brothers re-signed R.E.M. for a multi-million dollar fee.

AND THEN THERE WERE THREE

Bill Berry shocked fans by announcing his departure from R.E.M. in 1997, and retired to his farm in Georgia. Given his recent health scare, perhaps it was not that surprising. R.E.M. considered calling it a day, but instead they hired the best session musicians to embellish their next record, 'Up'. Many fans deserted R.E.M. after 'Up', but the band tried to woo them back with 'Reveal' in 2001, which was a magnificent return to form.

21

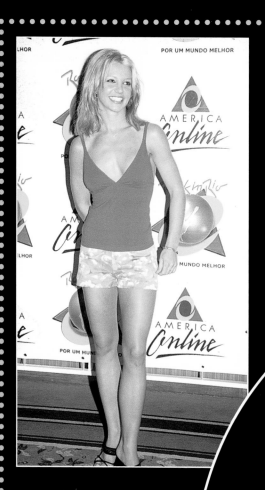

BRITNEY SPEARS

If you fed into a computer the ingredients needed to produce a '90s female pop star, the chances are it would come up with somebody remarkably similar to Britney Spears, a symbol of clean-cut American youth.

EARLY AMBITION

Britney has it all. A Californian tan, perfect gleaming teeth, a wide smile, a well-honed figure and a great voice have all put Britney right at the top of the pile. She was born in Los Angeles in 1981, and from a very early age she loved to dance, and sang with her local church choir. Ambitious from the start, Britney auditioned for the TV show 'The Mickey Mouse Club' when she was just eight years old. The producers were impressed and helped her to gain a place at a school for the performing arts.

DISNEY DIVA

'The Mickey Mouse Club' was ready for Britney by the time she was eleven, and she appeared on the show for two seasons, and featured in a number of TV commercials. But singing was Britney's first love, and in 1999 Jive Records released her first album, 'Baby One More Time'.

Britney uses a headset microphone to free up her hands.

Britney has co-written a novel with her mother Lynne.

'Baby One More Time' 1999

'Oops!...I Did It Again' 2000

DERBYSHIRE

SAINT BENEDICT SCHOOL

MUSIC TELEVISION

MTV was founded in 1981 as a channel for pop videos. Today, it's almost unheard of for a new pop song not to be accompanied by an expensive video, but back then videos were quite a novelty. Record companies realise that, however catchy a song might be, it will get nowhere without heavy video airplay on MTV and other channels, such as VH1.

Britney Spears has won several MTV awards.

BRITNEY DOES IT AGAIN

Britney was just 18 when the album entered the US chart at No. 1. It produced a string of radio-friendly hits, including the title track, '(You Drive Me) Crazy' and 'From The Bottom Of My Broken Heart', and became the best-selling album ever by a teenage girl. Britney's huge success paved the way for dozens of imitators, notably Christina Aguilera, and Britney was only too aware that she had to stay ahead of the game if her career was going to last. She returned with a more mature, raunchy image for her 2000 album 'Oops!...I Did it Again'.

SPICE GIRLS

Record companies and managers have been manufacturing pop groups for decades, but the idea of the Spice Girls was pure genius. Take five young women, each of them flamboyant and attractive in different ways, add some catchy pop songs and a large dose of attitude, and you have a hit-making formula. But despite appearances, the Spice Girls were no overnight success.

GETTING WHAT THEY REALLY, REALLY WANTED

Victoria Adams, Melanie Brown, Emma Bunton, Melanie Chisholm and Geri Halliwell were all active on the British modelling and theatrical circuit when they answered an advertisement for 'five lively girls' to form a new singing group in 1993. The manager who chose the lucky five was soon ditched, after the girls decided they would rather run their own careers, and for the next two years they struggled to secure a record contract. Most labels insisted that one of them should stand out as the group's leader, but the girls rejected the idea. Eventually, signed to Virgin, and teamed with new manager Simon Fuller and songwriter Elliot Kennedy, they released their first single, 'Wannabe', in 1996. It entered the chart at No. 1 – a first for a girl group.

'Spice' 1996

'Spiceworld' 1997
'Forever' 2000

The Spice Girls quickly became multi-millionaires.

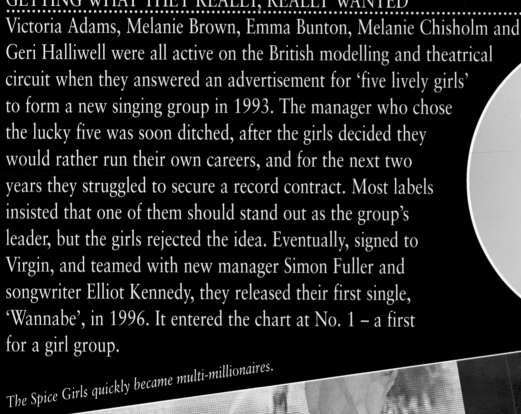

STANDING OUT

The girls each adopted a memorable identity. Victoria was Posh Spice, Emma was Baby, Mel B. was Scary, Mel C. was Sporty and Geri was Ginger Spice. The group immediately captured the imagination of the public and press alike, and they were rarely out of the charts in Britain, America and all over the world.

The Spice Girls were a major live attraction.

FIVE BECOME FOUR

The hit movie 'Spiceworld' capitalized on their success, but rifts were beginning to emerge. Simon Fuller was the first to go, and in May 1998, Geri left the group to pursue a successful solo career. The remaining four girls surprised many by opting to continue, and completed a successful world tour. Mel B. started a family, as did Victoria, who married the football ace David Beckham, and all four girls launched solo careers – critics dubbed Mel C. 'Talented Spice' after the release of her acclaimed album 'Northern Star'. The Spice Girls' publicity machine insists that the four remain best friends, but as they and their fans grow up, it's difficult to see how they can repeat their 1990s successes in the new millennium.

GIRL POWER

The Spice Girls were as much about rebellion and attitude as music, and they are still experts at filling up newspaper columns. They coined the expression 'girl power', and promoted themselves as strong, independent women. The craze for girl power spread to school playgrounds all over Britain, where young girls were now more likely to be seen practising martial arts than skipping rope. The group even announced that ex-Prime Minister Margaret Thatcher was the original Spice Girl, even though she was born way back in 1925!

The Spice Girls helped to launch Channel 5 on UK television in 1997.

SUEDE

Along with Blur, Suede pioneered the Britpop sound of the early 1990s, rejecting the dance-pop music which had dominated the British charts in the years before. The band was formed by two schoolmates.

GUITARIST WANTED

Singer Brett Anderson and bass guitarist Mat Osmon formed Geoff in 1985, and though the band soon fell apart, the pair remained friends and dreamed of fronting a serious group one day. At university in London four years later, they advertised in the rock magazine NME for a guitarist. Bernard Butler responded and the three started writing and recording. An early demo tape, 'Specially Suede' won the band a contest on BBC local radio, and an independent record contract with RML.

'Suede' 1993
'Dog Man Star' 1994

'Coming Up' 1996
'Head Music' 1999

'Coming Up' gave Suede five top 10 singles.

SETTLING DOWN

Brett's girlfriend Justine Frischmann joined Suede as second guitarist, and Mike Joyce, formerly of the Smiths filled the drum stool. Unfortunately Suede fell out with RML, and after another year simply rehearsing, Mike was replaced by Simon Gilbert and Justine left to form Elastica. The new four-piece Suede gained a strong reputation, and was hailed by Melody Maker magazine as the best new band in Britain, even though they hadn't released a record.

TROUBLE AHEAD

A contract with Nude Records finally gave Suede the chance to record some singles and an album. A UK tour was a great success, and 'Suede' became the fastest selling debut album of the early '90s. The lucrative American market beckoned.

LOST OPPORTUNITY

Sadly, Bernard's father died as the band was trying to crack the States, forcing the cancellation of their second tour. The band even had to change its name in America to the London Suede, owing to legal action by an obscure singer called Suede.

Brett Anderson is a provocative and suggestive performer.

Back in the studio, Bernard and Brett frequently quarrelled, and Bernard left the band near the end of the sessions for 'Dog Man Star'.

INSTANT FAME

Bernard was replaced by 17-year-old Richard Oakes, who found himself in the unusual position of having to perform the new album on stage, even though he had not appeared on it. The band added a keyboard-player, and built up a loyal fan base through the rest of the '90s, but Stateside success still eluded them. Without those early squabbles and problems on tour, who knows how huge Suede could have been?

TAKE THAT

Many groups have rashly claimed to be 'the biggest band since the Beatles', but in the case of Take That it's a justified description. As far as sales of singles were concerned, it's probably true that Take That sold more than any English act since the '60s. The group fired up hysteria amongst their teenage fans which is rarely seen – and made some great music too.

FIVE WHOLESOME BOYS

Take That was conceived as the British answer to New Kids on the Block, an American boy band which had taken the charts by storm in the late '80s. Manager Nigel Martin Smith approached Gary Barlow, Mark Owen and Robbie Williams, who sang together in the Cutest Rush, and teamed them with break-dancers Howard Donald and Jason Orange to form Take That in 1990. An independent single 'Do What U Like', accompanied by a raunchy video, launched the group in 1991.

SOLO SUCCESS

No one pinned much hope on Robbie Williams's chances of success after he left Take That. His weight ballooned, and he has talked openly about his problems with drugs and alcohol at the time. But Robbie made an astonishing comeback in the late '90s. He has captured the hearts of the British people and sold millions of copies of his singles 'Angels', 'Millennium' and 'Rock DJ', and his albums 'The Ego Has Landed' and 'Sing When You're Winning'. Who says the British don't love a winner?

Robbie Williams is one of the most talented singers in Britain, but has yet to make it in America.

Gary's solo career has never really taken off.

BACK FOR GOOD

Take That's early singles were mostly cover versions, but the need for new material prompted Gary Barlow to start writing himself. 'Back For Good' was a sensitive ballad, which won acclaim from fans and critics.

'Take That And Party' 1992
'Everything Changes' 1993

'Nobody Else' 1995
'Greatest Hits' 1996

REBEL

Gary's songwriting skills set him apart from the rest of the band, and rumours of a split started to take hold. Robbie, long held to be the 'bad boy' of the band, was noticeably quiet on their third album, and departed in 1995. He threw himself into a life of partying and heavy drinking, and was widely dismissed as a has-been by critics. How wrong they were!

GONE FOR GOOD

Gary's management was eager to groom him for a long career as a solo singer and songwriter, and the the rest of Take That felt disenchanted. Ironically, the band was unravelling just as 'Back For Good' was giving it long-awaited American success. Take That finally disbanded in February 1996.

Take That released their 'Greatest Hits' after they split.

GAZETTEER

At the start of the 1990s, there was a lot of pessimism about the future of pop music. The newspapers were full of stories about how youngsters no longer listened to records, preferring computer games instead. But good music never goes out of fashion, and the following acts helped to keep it alive.

Supergrass was formed in Oxford.

Sharleen Spiteri was once a hairdresser.

TALENTED TRIO

Supergrass was the sound of summer in 1995 with their top 3 hit 'Alright'. This pop song never hinted at the group's heavy sound on the albums 'I Should Coco' and 'In It For The Money'. The Scottish band Texas was in the doldrums for years after their 1989 hit 'I Don't Want A Lover', but singer Sharleen Spiteri was determined to return to the top. She enjoyed a remarkable comeback with 'White On Blonde' in 1997, and Texas is now one of Britain's top bands. Echobelly was formed in 1992. The band was touted as another Oasis after its debut album in 1994, but legal problems stalled its career in 1997, and everything went quiet for a while. It remains to be seen if they can enjoy a Texas-style revival.

Christina Aguilera performed for President Clinton.

Echobelly returned in 2001 after a four-year gap.

AMERICAN BOY BAND

Boy bands weren't just popular in Britain. Backstreet Boys were America's answer to Take That. Their first album sold 13 million copies, and the second sold a million in its first week.

Suede supported Dolores O'Riordan (right) and the Cranberries on a US tour.

Backstreet Boys were named best newcomers of 1995.

GIRL POWER

Salt 'N' Pepa was the biggest female hip-hop group of the decade. They hit No. 1 in 1994 with their third album 'Very Necessary'. Dolores O'Riordan fronts the Cranberries from Ireland, who became one of the most popular acts in America after they released 'Linger', taken from their first album in 1993. B*Witched, also from Ireland, was the youngest girl group to hit No. 1. And Christina Aguilera challenged Britney Spears for the title of top teen pop diva.

Salt 'N' Pepa has won numerous awards.

*B*Witched is Ireland's biggest girl group.*

INDEX